Alia and Essam

A Poetic Play

To watch the play, please scan the following QR Code:
Alia and Essam

Dr. Sultan bin Muhammad Al-Qasimi

Alia and Essam

A Poetic Play

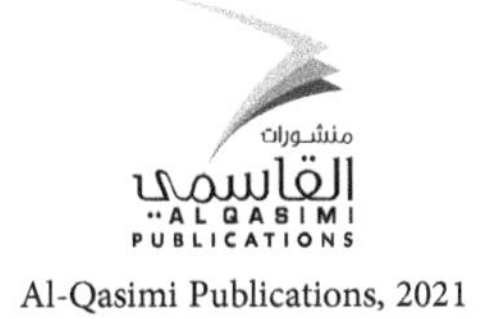

Al-Qasimi Publications, 2021

Book Title: Alia and Essam A Poetic Play (Play)
First published in 2015 in Arabic as "Alia wa Essam"
by : Al-Qasimi Publications
Author: Dr. Sultan bin Muhammad Al-Qasimi (United Arab Emirates)
Publisher Name: Al-Qasimi Publications
Sharjah, United Arab Emirates
Edition: First
Year of publication: 2021

Translated from the Arabic by: Dr. Ahmed Ali

ISBN: 978-9948-469-51-3
Printing Permission: National Media Council, Abu Dhabi, UAE
No. MC 01-03-4192526, Date: 05-08-2021

Age Classification: E
The age group that matches the content of the books was classified according to the age classification issued by the National Council for Media
----
Al- Qasimi Publications, Al Tarfa, Sheikh Mohammed Bin Zayed Road
PO Box 64009 Sharjah, United Arab Emirates
Tel: 0097165090000, Fax: 0097165520070
Email: info@aqp.ae

CONTENTS

Cast of Characters

- The Narrator
- The Arabian Knights of the Rula Tribe
- Alia
- Essam
- Essam's Mother
- Two Groups of Horsemen
- Alia's Father (Corpse)

Place

The Rula Tribe Quarters in the Desert between Hamat and Syria

Scene I

The camping site of the Arab Rula Tribe, a single black tent in the desert, not too far away from the audience.

The narrator tells the tale of Alia and Essam. Tribesmen on their horses pass by the tent. Then appear young Alia and Essam driving their sheep to the grazing area.

The Narrator:

The Rula Arabs favour tents to palaces
Hamat and Syria are their living quarters
They mount their steeds in victorious conquests
And live proudly as the bravest of fighters.

Chasing their enemies is their passion
One's glory is in spear and arrow
Fearless they march in a proud fashion
They dread no road, wide or narrow.

Only the orphans would behind stay
With the newborn who need love and care.
The tale I am narrating to you today
Is about Alia and Essam whose breed is rare.

As shepherds they grew, characters flawless
Like true Arabs, not in the least clueless.

Scene II

Alia appears with her hijab on. Essam, a grown-up young man holds her hand. They both come to the front of the tent.

The Narrator:

There they come, hand in hand
Love has joined their hearts together
In the vigour of youth they both stand
Their fate is tied, one to the other.

The young woman has veiled her beauty
She was a flower at blossom peak
A bundle of joy, pride and modesty;
Not a commodity for all to peek.

And our Essam is a sight to behold
Strong, proud, a true man of honour
Made for greatness, he's been told
Look at his sword, he shakes it in valour.

His mother has called on him today
Let's hear what she has to say.

The Mother:

Essam, my son, my pride and joy!

Alia leaves.
The Mother appears holding a sword and a shield.

The Mother:

How I longed for this day to come!
Here, my son, take these as a foy.

You've now grown brave and wise
The whole tribe looks up to you
But soon they will look in despise
Respect and honour will be lost, too.

Your father's life would be in vain
If his death you do not avenge.

Go, my son, bring solace, end pain,
Nothing is sweeter than revenge.

Essam:

My father? Murdered? Pray, do tell
Who had dared, my father, to kill?
A courageous man who never fell
In battle, in raid, but betrayed still?!

I swear by all that is mighty and holy
My father's enemy is now mine
My patience is running thin and truly
Do tell whom it was the treacherous swine!

The Mother:

Alia's father is the vexing fiend
Brought us misery, tears and sadness
Take this sword, take this shield,
Let the tribe behold and witness.

The Narrator:

Essam so hurriedly rode his mare,
Left his mother; his heart so sad

The pain was more than he could bear
How could he kill his beloved's dad?!

But as fate will have it, he sees the man
Riding a steed, running a course
Away he was from kin and clan
A worthy opponent on a mighty horse.

A duel takes place to the side of the tent.

The Narrator:

Here are the fighters; their eyes meet
They both could read each other's mind
The dust is raised under the horses' feet
Blows are thrown, front and behind

Essam repeatedly his opponent stabbed
Broke his bones with force and might
Left him dead; his horse he grabbed.
Home he went as he won the fight.

He shouted: "Mother, the deed is done."

The mother comes hurriedly as she hears his voice.

Essam:

The deed is done; the deed is done.

Alia appears next to her father's corpse.
She then rushes to Essam.

Scene III

The Narrator:

Jubilant they were with revenge and win

Then Alia arrived, with spirit defeated

Her smile gone, her face bleeding,

The same call she made and repeated:

Alia crying:

Essam ....

The mother leaves and enters the tent.

Alia:

Essam, my love, my father is killed

You must avenge him, you must do so

You cannot leave my wish unfulfilled
Who else can end my grief and sorrow?

Essam:

Sweetheart, revenge you soon will hear
I will heal your aching heart
You must not wail or shed a tear
Your father's killer I will tear apart.

The Narrator:

And before he uttered another word
He pulled his sword, his heart he stabbed
The scene was brutal and so absurd
That Alia lost her mind and grabbed

The same sword and tore her heart
Shouting …

Alia:

…. Death will not do us part;
Don't leave my love, for me do wait
In death we join our destined fate.

www.ingramcontent.com/pod-product-compliance
Ingram Content Group UK Ltd.
Pitfield, Milton Keynes, MK11 3LW, UK
UKHW021959190726
13853UKWH00004B/1615

9 789948 469513